Please Don't Say Hello

by Phyllis Gold

Photographs by Carl Baker

Photographic Conceptualization by Phyllis Gold

Library of Congress Catalog Number 74-13185
ISBN: 0-87705-211-5
Copyright © 1975 by Human Sciences Press, a division of Behavioral Publications, Inc., 72 Fifth Avenue, New York, New York 10011

Printed in the United States of America
56789 987654321

For their cooperation in the creation of this book, the author wishes to thank: the Suffolk Child Development Center in Bay Shore, Long Island; her friends who portrayed the people of Westwood Drive; and the professional model, Russell Davis, who portrayed Eddie.

Library of Congress Cataloging in Publication Data

Gold, Phyllis.
    Please don't say hello.

    SUMMARY: With the support and love of his family, and through them the neighborhood children, a nine-year-old autistic boy is able to emerge from his shell.
    [1. Autism—Fiction]   I. Baker, Carl, illus.
II. Title.
PZ7.G5633Pl   [Fic]   74-13185

Foreword

This gentle story of the playmates of a handicapped boy brought tears to the eyes of the teacher with whom I first shared it. Other readers will be moved by it, especially those who can appreciate the skill with which the author has translated the mystique surrounding the word "autism" into the everyday world of childhood.

Professionals have clung too long to the past in labelling autism both rare and hopeless. They carry a heavy burden of blame for the confusion in diagnosis and management which has excluded too many children with autistic symptoms from their families, their schools, and their playmates.

It is parents who have recognized that autism is a group of symptoms, not a disease. It is parents who have urged researchers to attend to the clues which will shed light on the several causes of autism.

It is parents who have fought long and valiantly for access to education as the path of hope for their children.

Parents and teachers of all mentally handicapped children will be grateful to the sensitive parent-author of *Please Don't Say Hello* for her reminder that all children with autism can learn. Younger readers will be helped to learn to accept a child with autism as a friend.

—Mary Stewart Goodwin, M.D.

For Paul, Liz and especially Mitch

Meeting the New Family

It was summer. It was a different kind of day for the children of Westwood Drive. A moving van drove up the street and parked, and the children watched as the men unloaded the massive, clamoring truck. When a car drove up, Billy, Alan, Jimmy and Charlie gathered around, excited to meet the family who was moving into the new house.

The new people got out of the car. There was a tall, dark-haired man, an attractive blonde lady, a pretty girl with straight blonde hair who looked about seventeen, and a boy their own age. The lady

said, "Hello, We are the Masons." The new boy said, "And I'm Paul. Do you live on this street too?"

The children nodded and said, "Yes," and then Paul's mother said something to him, very quietly, and after that the Mason family went into their new house. All except Paul.

Paul was very friendly. He noticed Billy was bouncing a basketball and said, "There's a hoop in my back yard. It must have belonged to the people who lived here before. Do you want to play?"

The children chorused, "Yes!"

Then Paul said, "Okay. Just wait a minute."

Paul walked toward his family's car, which was parked near the driveway, and then around the car toward the door on the other side. Meanwhile the children peered in through the opposite

window. There was a boy sitting in there, staring straight ahead. He looked a little younger than Paul. He had golden blonde hair, sparkling blue eyes, and glowing smooth skin. He was very good-looking. He did not turn his head to look at all the children.

Paul opened the car door on the side where the boy was sitting. He said, "Come out now. It's all right." But the boy didn't look at Paul either. He continued to stare straight ahead as though nobody were there.

Paul reached into the car and touched the boy's arm. Again he spoke softly to him. "Don't be afraid," he told him. "Please come out." The boy made an odd, almost indescribable sound: "Ehhhhhhh, ehhhhhhhh." Then he covered his eyes by pushing the backs of his hands hard against them and very slowly climbed out of the car. Once outside, he just looked straight ahead, as though

there were a window out there that he was gazing through.

Paul told the children, "This is my brother Eddie."

The children said, "Hello, Eddie." But Eddie behaved as though the children weren't even there. He didn't look at them or answer.

Jimmy asked, "Can't he talk?"

Billy asked, "Is he deaf, or blind?"

Alan told Billy, "Of course he isn't deaf. Didn't you see he heard Paul when he told him to come out of the car? And I saw him look at me, quickly, out of the corner of his eye, so he isn't blind, either."

"Eddie can see and he can hear," Paul agreed, "and he does talk . . . sometimes."

At that moment Eddie sat down on one of the steps before the front walk leading to the house. He opened his right fist so that something dropped out of his hand. The children came closer to see what it was. There were three metal coins that looked almost like real money.

Charlie asked Paul, "Why does he have that?"

Paul answered, "Eddie carries it around with him."

"Why?" asked Billy.

"Watch," Paul told them.

Eddie took the largest coin and stood it on its side. He gave it a toss and started it spinning around. Then he took the coin next largest in size and did the same with that one. Then he did the same thing with the smallest, until all the coins were spinning at once. And by giving each coin another twist every few seconds, he kept all the coins spinning together. The children were just amazed!

"Boy!" said Jimmy.

"Wow, look what he's doing!" shouted Alan.

"How does he do it?" they all wanted to know.

Paul said, "Oh, Eddie can do some unusual things."

Eddie let the coins stop spinning, picked them up and put them in his pocket. And then he did something very very strange. While still sitting, he pushed himself onto the grass. He made those eerie sounds again, "Ehhhhhhhh, ehhhhhhhh." Then, with his legs off the ground and his knees slightly bent, he began to turn his body around in a circle.

He twirled himself around once, and then again. First slowly, then a little faster . . . until he was spinning himself around and around very rapidly. Now the children were just astounded!

Charlie giggled. He said, "Look! Eddie is pretending he's a top!"

"No, I think he's being an airplane," Jimmy said confidently.

Alan asked, "What is Eddie doing?"

Paul tried to explain. "Eddie isn't making believe; he doesn't know how. He just likes to spin things, that's all. He likes to spin himself around, too. Sometimes he whirls himself around while he's standing up."

"But why?" the children asked, all together.

Paul answered "I don't know exactly, but I think it makes him feel better."

Alan asked, "What wrong with him, anyway? He's weird. I think he's a retard."

"Eddie's not retarded," Paul said, and he looked a little angry. "Sometimes he's very smart. I mean, he can do some things I can't even do and I'll bet none of you can either."

Alan asked, "You mean like spinning that money? That isn't so smart."

"He can do some things that are smarter than that," Paul responded.

Eddie stopped spinning himself and made his strange noise, "Ehhhhhhhh, ehhhhhhhh." Then he began to stare straight ahead again, as though he was looking at something out there that no one else could see. The children crowded around Eddie.

Alan told him, "I don't think you can really do smart things. I don't even believe you can talk. If you CAN talk, SAY SOMETHING." Eddie covered his eyes again with the backs of his hands, and now he again made his peculiar noises, "Ehhhhhhhh, ehhhhhhhh."

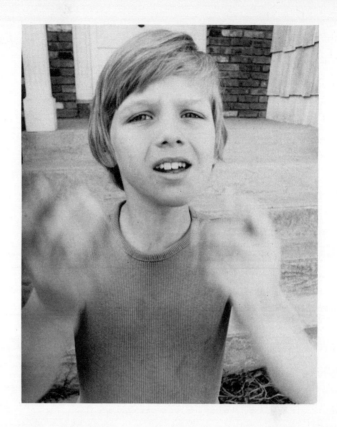

"Stop it!" Paul told Alan. "You're frightening him!"

But Alan went even closer to Eddie. "TALK!" he shouted at Eddie. "SAY something!"

Eddie stood up. He began to flap his hands in a way Alan and the other children had never seen before. Eddie waved his hands straight up and down in front of his chin, very rapidly, as though he were trying to shake something off of them. And then he did talk. In a hollow, flat kind of voice that sounded like a robot's, he said, "Don't say hello." And then, still flapping his hands in that strange manner, he began to run. He ran across the front

lawn, up the front steps, and pushed open the door
to his house. And as he slammed the door shut, the
children could hear him moaning, "Ehhhhhhhh,
ehhhhhhhh."

"Eddie's afraid, and you've made him even
more afraid," Paul told Alan angrily.

"What is he afraid of?" asked Billy.

Paul replied, "Eddie is afraid of this place because it's new. And he's afraid of all of you. And
sometimes Eddie is just afraid."

"Why won't he look at us?" Jimmy asked.
"Why won't he say hello?"

Paul answered, "I don't think he can."

In the Mason's Back Yard

The following day it was warm and the sun was shining. All the children were invited to the Mason's back yard for a barbeque and a swim in the pool. The children of Westwood Drive liked Paul, his sister Lizbeth, and Mr. and Mrs. Mason, and had a wonderful time at their house.

Every day that week they came back to play. They played basketball, they swam in the pool, and they watched Eddie. Eddie was different from any boy they had ever seen before. He was an unusual boy; strange, but also quite amazing.

The children could see that Eddie was like them in many ways. When the Good Humor truck came around Eddie liked to get ice cream just the way they did. But Eddie would eat only one kind. The only kind he wanted was a raspberry-flavored double popsicle. He would pull the popsicle apart and eat the two parts separately. Soon they noticed that whenever the truck came along Eddie would tug on one of the children's arms, and they all learned that meant Eddie wanted them to buy him a popsicle.

One day Jimmy bought Eddie a single raspberry-flavored popsicle, because the Good Humor man didn't have the double ones that day. But when Eddie saw it, he got terribly upset and started to flap his hands, screaming "Ehhhhhhhh, ehhhhhhhh."

Jimmy tried to make him feel better. "It tastes exactly the same as the other kind, Eddie," he said. But Eddie was still upset. He wouldn't even taste the popsicle. "Ehhhhhhhh, ehhhhhhhh," he cried again, then threw the popsicle to the ground.

Jimmy was annoyed that Eddie could be so silly. But Paul told him, "Eddie gets disturbed when things are changed. I think when that happens he feels more confused."

Eddie also liked to play with the basketball sometimes. One day in the back yard he had a really good game of catch with his father; he threw and caught the ball very well, even though a lot of the time he wasn't even looking at the ball, but at something else entirely. Mr. Mason explained that Eddie often had trouble concentrating on one thing at a time, and that was why he didn't seem to pay attention to the ball.

And Eddie loved the pool just as the other children did, but he only liked to go splash in the water when he could be there alone. If one of the other children jumped into the pool, Eddie would get out and go sit alone, with his back to the other children. He would sit that way staring at nothing, or at least at nothing anybody else could see. Or, he would sit for a long time just spinning his coins.

Eddie certainly did talk, as Paul had claimed, but it was a different way of talking. He spoke in one tone, without much inflection, as if he were running out of energy. He sounded something like a phonograph that someone had turned off with the needle still on the record; you could hear the sound getting slower and slower, as if it might stop any minute.

And sometimes it sounded—at least Paul explained it that way—as if Eddie wasn't quite sure who he was. He never called himself "I," and when he wanted a drink of water he said, "*You* want some water" rather than "I want some water." He never answered a question with yes; if his mother asked, "Eddie, do you want some water?" he would reply, "*You* want some water." That was Eddie's way of saying yes. It was very fascinating and confusing.

But the children of Westwood Drive learned that Paul had been right when he said that Eddie could do some really smart things that even they couldn't do. They first found this out one day when all the children were sitting in the back yard and Paul suddenly asked,

"Eddie, what is the capital of Poland?"

Eddie answered, without even having to stop and think, "The capital of Poland is Warsaw." And he didn't stop there. In his robot-like voice Eddie continued, "The capital of Greece is Athens, the capital of Switzerland is Bern . . ." Eddie went on and on, naming more countries of the world and

their capitals than the other children had even heard
of. Which is a rather intelligent thing for a nine-
year old boy to be able to do.

And Eddie did other things the rest of the children of Westwood Drive couldn't do. One day he
sat outside at the picnic table and without any help
from anyone, rapidly did a 500-piece jigsaw puzzle
with the picture face down. The other children were
amazed!

And Eddie loved machines, and drew great pictures of robots and computers.

The children asked Lizbeth, Eddie's older sister, "How come there are some things that are so easy that Eddie cannot do, but he can do some things that are so hard?"

Lizbeth thought for a while and then answered, "I think for all of us some things are easier and some things harder to do. For Eddie it's even more that way."

One afternoon the children were very busy playing with a frisbe in the Mason's back yard, and suddenly, when he thought nobody was watching him, Eddie picked up the basketball which had been lying on the grass. He threw it into the basket, and then he did it two more times without missing.

Charlie shouted, "Hey! Look what Eddie did!"

Jimmy said, "Do it again, Eddie."

Eddie took the ball and ran toward the woods in back of the basketball court. Paul yelled, "Oh no, he's going to throw it into the woods, down that hill," and ran to catch up with him, with the other children following quickly behind. Paul reached Eddie's side, but too late to stop him; Eddie threw the ball far into the woods in back of the house.

Paul was very angry. He told Eddie, "That was wrong. Go get the ball." But Eddie turned his back and walked away from the other children. He sat down on the patio and began to spin his coins. The children were angry at Eddie for throwing their ball into the woods, but Paul explained, "Eddie didn't want us to know what he can do; I guess he's afraid then we might expect him to play with us and that he won't know how. He's angry that he can't do what we can, and I think that's why he threw the ball into the woods."

18

Well, the children of Westwood Drive had never met a boy like Eddie! A boy who did such strange things, yet such smart things too. A boy who could throw baskets but couldn't play ball with them. A boy who could name the capitals of most of the countries of the world but didn't know how to ask for a glass of water the right way. A boy who wouldn't say hello.

A few days later Alan, Jimmy and Charlie came into the Mason's back yard to play with Paul, and Paul came outside to greet them. But he noticed one of the children was missing and asked, "Where's Billy?"

Charlie said, "I don't think he can play here anymore."

"Why not?" Paul asked.

And Charlie said, "His mother and father told him he can't play with you anymore. Because your brother Eddie is crazy."

Paul looked as though he were going to cry. Then he walked into his house, and very soon came back out again. This time Mrs. Mason and Lizbeth were with him.

Mrs. Mason told the children, "Very soon we'll invite all your mothers and fathers here one evening, and while they are here we'll explain about Eddie."

"Is Eddie really crazy?" Charlie asked. "What is wrong with him?"

Mrs. Mason said, "I have an idea. There's some ice cream in the freezer. I think I'll get us some and while we're eating it we can talk about Eddie."

Learning about Autism

So that summer day, sitting on the stone steps in the Mason's back-yard garden, Mrs. Mason told the children of Westwood Drive about Eddie. She said, "Sometimes Eddie gets excited and afraid, and other times he acts like he's in a world of his own. Eddie feels very confused inside."

Charlie asked, "You mean like I felt the day I got lost at the zoo and was afraid I wouldn't be able to get home?"

"Maybe something similar to that," Mrs. Mason replied, "except Eddie often feels confused

and afraid when nothing is happening to give him reason to. Things inside Eddie are making him feel that way. Eddie knows he is different and doesn't understand why. He knows other children think he's peculiar. He is hurt when they tease him. He can't say all that, but he feels it."

Just as Mrs. Mason finished her sentence the children could hear the ring of the telephone from inside the house, and Mrs. Mason got up to answer it. "Lizbeth can tell you more about Eddie while I'm gone," she said.

Charlie repeated the question he'd asked before. "*Is* Eddie crazy?" he asked.

Lizbeth, sounding a little angry, answered, "Calling Eddie 'crazy,' or any other name, isn't nice. It's cruel. Eddie is sick. Some doctors call what Eddie has autism or infantile autism, and children with Eddie's kind of sickness are autistic."

"Why do they call them that?" Alan wanted to know. "Is that because they can all draw pictures, like Eddie?"

"Oh, no," Lizbeth replied, smiling slightly. "Not all autistic children can draw or do just the same things Eddie can. 'Artistic' *sounds* something like autistic, but they are not at all the same thing. The word autistic comes from the Greek word auto, which means 'self.' So, autistic means these are children who are within themselves, who have trouble getting outside of themselves enough to get along with other people in what would be considered the normal way."

Charlie asked, "Does that mean there are a lot of children who act just like Eddie?"

Lizbeth said, "Nobody is just like Eddie. All autistic children are different from each other just as all of you are not exactly the same."

Mrs. Mason came out of the house just then, and as she again sat down with Lizbeth and the children she added, "It is true, though, that many autistic children do have a number of the same, or similar, behaviors in common. Many of them spin objects or whirl themselves around, shake their hands or wiggle their fingers in various ways, have ways of talking and moving which may seem peculiar; some don't speak at all. Many, like Eddie, don't like things to be changed and like to have things done in the same particular way. Most autistic children have unusual fears, too."

Jimmy said, "Last year I had chicken pox and none of my friends were allowed to visit me then. Maybe that's why Billy's mother and father won't let him come here. Can we catch what Eddie has?"

"There is no way anybody can catch what Eddie has," Lizbeth assured him.

"Isn't there any medicine that will make Eddie better?" asked Jimmy. "When I had chicken pox the doctor gave me medicine, and that made me feel much better. And soon I was all better."

"Yes," Charlie said, "Why don't you take Eddie to a doctor and get him medicine that will make him well?"

Mrs. Mason explained, "Eddie has been to lots of doctors. The doctor he goes to now has given him pills that make him feel a lot better. They seem to make him feel more relaxed. But the doctor can't cure Eddie because nobody is positive, yet, what caused his sickness and how to cure it. Scientists are studying and doing research to find out a lot more. These scientists think now that autistic children are born with their handicap, just as blind and deaf children are born with theirs. They believe something is physically wrong with them, something inside."

For a moment nobody said anything. Then Mrs. Mason went on. "You know," she told the children, "the human body is in many ways the most amazing and complicated machine there is. And just the way something wrong with a real machine can keep it from working right, some parts of a person's body can go wrong. With autistic children something did go wrong, and nobody yet has been able to discover what that is."

Charlie asked, "You mean, nothing can be done to help Eddie until they find out what is really wrong with him?"

"Eddie can't be cured yet," Mrs. Mason said, "but he can be helped. For example, Eddie goes to a special school where he lives during the school year. Otherwise it is very much like your school, except at Eddie's school they understand his special problems and know ways to help him. We hope the school will help him."

"But why does he live at school?" Alan asked. "Aren't there any schools for children with Eddie's problem where he could go on the bus every day and come home, the way we do?"

Mrs. Mason told the children, "Yes, there are those kind of schools. There is one about half-an-hour's ride from here, and it's a good school. But unfortunately there aren't enough of these schools yet, and this one didn't have room for Eddie just now. Anyway, we decided that right now it's better for Eddie to go to a school where he can live during the school year, since he has to be watched and kept occupied and helped so much of the time, not just during school hours. We felt this can be done better for Eddie right now at a school where he can live." She added, "Except . . . it would be better if there were a school like *that* closer to home, too. Because then we could see Eddie more often."

Alan asked, "Will they know what's wrong with Eddie soon and cure him? Will he be able to play basketball with us next summer?"

Lizbeth answered, slowly and a little sadly, "We don't know how Eddie will be next summer. That depends on many things. But you can all help Eddie, I think."

The children asked, "What can WE do?"

Lizbeth answered, "Well, don't tease Eddie. He has feelings just as you do, and if you tease him that makes him feel even worse about himself. Talk to him even though you don't expect him to answer; he may surprise you. Ask him if he wants to play with you. Even if he won't, he'll feel better knowing you'd like him to. And it's so important to always remember to try to understand and accept everyone who seems not quite like we are. To treat everybody as we would want to be treated."

The following night Mr. and Mrs. Mason invited Jimmy, Charlie, Alan and Billy's parents to their home for supper. They explained Eddie's condition to the mothers and fathers, too, just as they had to the children. And the next day, when Charlie, Jimmy and Alan came to play in the

Mason's back yard, Billy came too. Paul greeted Billy happily; he felt so much better now that Billy was allowed to play with him again.

For the rest of the summer the children did talk to Eddie, and they asked him to play with them. But when they handed him the basketball he would drop it or throw it into the woods. Even though Paul had explained why he did it, they couldn't help but feel angry. It was natural, of course, to feel angry, but they tried to remember what Lizbeth had said about understanding people and tried not to be too angry. And when they tried to talk to Eddie, he would still make that strange noise of his, "Ehhhhhhhh, ehhhhhhhh," or say, "Don't say hello." And go sit by himself, staring into space.

One day after Eddie had done this Alan said, "I don't think Eddie wants to play with us or ever will. I don't think he will ever talk to us, either." So after that, the children stopped trying as much to talk to Eddie, and they hardly ever asked him to play basketball or frisbe anymore. And that made Eddie feel even more alone and terribly sad.

Summer was over. The leaves on the trees would soon begin to turn red and yellow, and it was time to go back to school. Eddie watched through the window while Paul and his friends got on their bus and went off to their school. He felt very lonely.

Then the next day his mother and father drove him to his school far away.

And all winter the children of Westwood Drive went to school, went sleighriding and ice-skating, and did all the things most children do. And although Paul did still think about Eddie, the other children were much too busy to think of him at all.

Eddie's School

One day just before the start of June, the neighborhood children were playing basketball with Paul in the back yard. Charlie had just made a really difficult jump shot, and was a little upset when Mrs. Mason suddenly came out of the house and distracted everyone's attention from it. But when he found out why she had come out to talk to them, he was very excited. "I've got a surprise for you," she told the children.

"A surprise," Paul asked; "What kind of a surprise?"

"A very special kind of surprise, that you can't get anywhere else," his mother answered. "How would you all like to come with me to pick up Eddie at his school?"

The children thought it was a wonderful idea. They had never seen a school like Eddie's before, where the children lived all the time, and didn't go home to sleep every night. And they had never seen any other autistic children, either, and wondered whether they were like Eddie. "When can we go?" they all shouted at once.

"If your parents think it's a good idea, we'll go on Saturday," Mrs. Mason said.

Alan, Billy, Charlie and Jimmy got permission from their parents to go on the trip and arrived at the Mason's house right on time on Saturday morning. Then Lizbeth and Paul, Mr. and Mrs. Mason and Paul's four friends piled into the Mason's stationwagon and drove into the country to see Eddie's school.

It was a long drive, and as they looked out the window, counting cows and license plates, Mrs. Mason told them about the problems of finding schools for autistic children.

"First of all," she began, "There weren't any at all until a few years ago. People just didn't care enough or understand enough about what autistic children need to build special schools for them. And then there were finally schools, but only very small ones. Even now there aren't nearly enough schools, and many children can't get the special training and education they need."

"If there were more schools," asked Alan, "so that everyone who needed help could get it at just the right kind of school, would all autistic children get better?"

"Some autistic children would get well enough to go to public schools, or to special classes in public schools. But all autistic children are different, and some will always need extra help."

"And what about Eddie?" Alan asked. "Will he ever be normal?"

Mrs. Mason answered, "We can't really tell, now, how much Eddie is going to progress. That will depend on all sorts of things, like whether he will always have a good school to go to, whether scientists can discover some of the causes of autism, and whether other people around him want to accept and help him."

"That's what Lizbeth said once," said Jimmy. "She said if we were nice to Eddie, and asked him to play with us, we might be able to help him get better."

"That's right," Lizbeth said. "Every time you tried to get him to play with you last summer, it helped. It made him feel better."

"We'll help him some more this summer," said Jimmy excitedly, "and maybe he'll get even better!"

Soon they arrived at the school. Mrs. Wilson, the assistant director came out to meet them and offered to show them around. Inside, the children noticed how much Eddie's school looked like their own. It had the same long hallways, and classrooms with big windows overlooking the lawn. But inside each classroom they could see there were only a few children. This surprised the visitors, but Mrs. Wilson explained, "We have only four or five children in each class, with one teacher and one assistant teacher shared by two classes. The children need a lot of attention, and they learn best if there's not too much noise or confusion around them."

Mrs. Wilson led them into a classroom where there were several children working at their desks. They heard the teacher ask one boy, "How are you, Mark?"

Mark smiled and answered, "I'm fine." On Mark's desk were big sheets of paper with sentences

written on them that he had to complete, like:

My name is _____ . Date _____ .

Weather _____ . 12+7 = _____ .

16-7= _____ .

Mark seemed to be having a good time filling in the blanks. Every now and then he would look away and stare at nothing in particular, just the way Eddie did, and then the teacher would remind him to pay attention, and he'd go back to his work. He obviously enjoyed showing everybody how much he could do.

"Mark is ten, and came to the school about six years ago," Mrs. Wilson told the visitors. "He taught himself to read and write when he was three and a half!"

"He must be smart," Alan said. "Is he really autistic?"

"There's no doubt about that," said Mrs. Wilson. "Many autistic children are extremely bright. But they still have serious problems. Mark, for example, didn't like to eat when he first came here. He would only eat hard-boiled eggs and turkey—and then only the white meat. He used to talk so fast that no one could understand him, and often what he said made no sense at all. He would repeat words or phrases he'd heard somewhere, that didn't fit the situation at all.

"Mark also used to recite television commercials," Mrs. Wilson continued. "And if he saw an ad on television even once, he could sit down and draw it from memory, so exactly that it looked like a photograph. A few years ago Mark went to California with his family. They were advertising a gasoline there called Phillips 66, and for weeks afterward Mark would walk around repeating 'Phillips 66 gasoline.' He could also draw the trademark for the gasoline, even though he had seen it only once or twice on television. And he could draw it perfectly! So perfectly, in fact, that every line of it was exactly as wide as it had been on television."

"How could he do that?" Charlie asked, sounding a little as if he didn't really believe it.

Mrs. Wilson shrugged her shoulders. "We aren't really sure yet why some autistic children can do certain things so easily which would be very hard for other children to do."

Mark was still working quietly, counting with small wooden blocks as he did the arithmetic problems. "Mark never used to be able to sit so still," Mrs. Wilson said. "When he first came here, especially if something frightened him, like a strange noise, he used to run around, unable to stay in one place for more than a few seconds, as if something had suddenly broken loose inside him."

The Masons and their friends followed Mrs. Wilson back out into the hall. Jimmy wanted to know why Eddie never ran around like Mark. "How come Eddie sits still so much of the time, but Mark runs around?"

Mrs. Mason explained that while some autistic children are too active, others are withdrawn, like Eddie, and sometimes the same child will be, at different times, both overactive and withdrawn. "When an autistic child gets too active," she went on, "it isn't the same as when you and your friends get excited and run from one activity to the next. I guess I can explain it by saying that you would run from doing one thing to doing something else, while the autistic child would run from nothing to nothing—dash around but not really be accomplishing anything."

Mrs. Wilson led the visitors into another classroom, where they met Sarah, a very little girl who was drinking grape juice, and her teacher, Mrs. Johnson. Sarah looked up curiously at the children and watched them for a moment before going back to her grape juice.

"When Sarah came here about six months ago, she had trouble really looking at anything," Mrs. Johnson said. "She had a foggy look in her eyes most of the time."

Alan whispered to Mrs. Mason, "Does she mean like Eddie gets?" and Mrs. Mason nodded.

"We try to teach the children here to establish eye contact. This means helping them learn to look right at another person, rather than looking away, or looking down, the way many autistic children do," explained Mrs. Wilson.

Mrs. Johnson went to Sarah's desk. Holding Sarah's head lightly in her hands she told her, "Look at me Sarah." For a while Sarah looked somewhere else entirely. Then she turned toward Mrs. Johnson, who immediately gave her a piece of candy. But after a while she turned away again, and Mrs. Johnson said, "Look at me, Sarah," and again

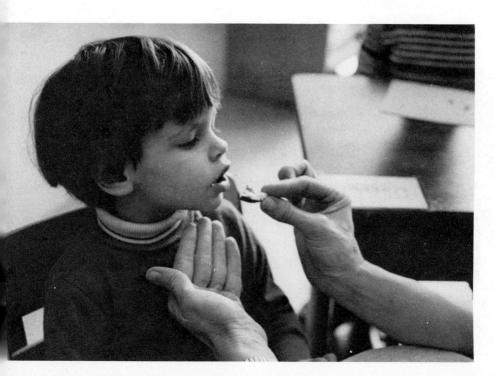

she hesitantly moved her head so that she was looking at Mrs. Johnson. This time she got a potato chip, which she ate happily.

"This is a way of helping children learn," Mrs. Wilson said. "Each time Sarah does what we ask her to, or even if she almost does it, or tries very hard, we give her something she likes—like candy, or potato chips—so that she knows that she's done something well. Gradually she learns that when she tries to behave in what we consider a normal way, she is rewarded for it. This is called behavior modification."

Now Sarah and Mrs. Johnson were playing with a puppet. Sarah seemed a little afraid of being touched, but by playing with the puppet and Mrs.

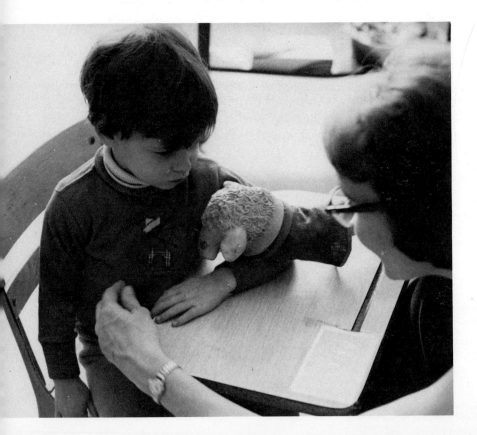

Johnson, who hugged her gently now and then, she learned how nice it was to be with other people and touch them. As the children left the classroom, Sarah looked up at them again and smiled.

"When Sarah first came here," Mrs. Wilson said, "she would stare at her fingers all the time, and wouldn't look directly at anyone."

"Why would she stare at her fingers?" asked Paul.

"Thats another question that we don't have an answer to yet. There are all sorts of theories. Many autistic children sometimes move their hands, or fingers, or legs in odd ways."

"Like Eddie's hand flapping," Paul suggested.

His mother nodded. "I've noticed that many autistic children seem confused about their bodies," Mrs. Mason said. "They don't quite understand who they are, and where all the parts of their body are located."

"Yes, I've noticed that too," agreed Mrs. Wilson. "But again, we don't really understand why."

"Isn't she awfully young to be in school?" Mr. Mason asked.

Mrs. Wilson answered, "She's certainly young. But it's important for autistic children to begin being helped when they are very young. This way they have a much greater chance of improving."

"Look! A playground!" Alan suddenly shouted, and pointed toward the door at the end of the hall, through which they could see an open space with swings, big blocks to climb on, and wooden, car-shaped rocking toys.

"Why don't we all go out and see it," suggested Mrs. Wilson, and the children all rushed down the hall and out the door, with the Masons following close behind.

Among the many children and teachers on the playground, the children recognized Mark and Sarah. They watched them play and noticed that Mark and Sarah, and the other children too, didn't play with each other, but stayed apart, each playing alone and not paying much attention to anyone else. They tended to wander from toy to toy, without actually doing much at all. Then one of the teachers came over and helped Sarah sit down in one of the rocking toys. She smiled happily as she moved back and forth.

A child they had noticed in one of the class-rooms walked by them slowly, and they saw that his walk was awkward and stiff. Many of the children they saw playing moved strangely, and they remembered that Mrs. Wilson had mentioned that this was quite common among autistic children.

Then Charlie suddenly asked, "Hey! Where did all the Masons go?"

They all looked around, and saw a little group clustered on the other side of the playground.

"Look! They've found Eddie!" said Jimmy. And they all ran to join Paul and his family.

Mrs. Mason was hugging Eddie, who seemed to enjoy all the attention he was getting. Then she let him go, and he turned to look at the children.

"Hi, Eddie," they all said. Eddie didn't answer, but he didn't look away either.

Summertime Again

That summer the children noticed some ways in which Eddie had changed and others in which he was still exactly the same. He hardly ever spinned himself around any more, and he didn't flap his hands as much either. Often he seemed more interested in watching what the other children were doing than in spinning his coins. And now when the Good Humor truck came, he surprised everyone by saying, "*I* want ice cream." Every once in a while he would call himself "you," the way he used to, but more often he said "I."

One day after Eddie had been in the pool Mrs. Mason asked, "Did you have a good time swimming?"

Eddie answered, "Yes!" and the children were all very excited because they had never heard him answer a question with the word yes before.

Alan asked, "What has happened to make Eddie change?"

Mrs. Mason answered, "Many things might have helped—the school where Eddie has been receiving help, the help our family has given him, too, and maybe just the fact that Eddie's getting older and a little more mature." And she added, "I also think all you children did something very important, which may have helped Eddie a lot. You did try to be nice to him. I think that made him feel better about being with other children, and better about himself."

But there were times when Eddie disappointed the children. The very next day they were playing ball and wanted Eddie to join in. "Here Eddie, you throw it," said Jimmy handing him the ball. But Eddie threw the ball into the woods and walked away. He went into the pool, alone, for just a minute, and then came out and sat down and just stared that faraway stare as he used to.

The children were disappointed. Alan said disgustedly, "I thought Eddie was getting better, but look; he's doing the same old things."

Paul told them, "Well, Eddie will still have good and bad days. Nobody changes completely overnight, you know. Maybe tomorrow he'll have a better day."

And that summer when the children played ball, Eddie didn't always walk away by himself anymore. Once in a while he did, but most of the time now he'd stand nearby and watch. He went into the pool the same time as the other children did, that summer, and seemed not to be afraid. And all that summer the children talked to Eddie. And asked him to play. And hoped that he would.

Once again the summer was ending. Soon it would be time for the children of Westwood Drive to go back to school. And for Eddie to return to his school far away.

One breezy afternoon, a few days before school was to begin again, the children were having a game of basketball. Eddie was standing nearby, watching.

Suddenly Charlie took the ball and gave it to Eddie, and said, "Here. This time you throw it into the basket."

Eddie took the ball. The children watched expectantly. It looked like Eddie was going to do it. But Eddie dropped the ball, turned and walked away.

The children were so disappointed. Alan said, "I'm going to tell you something. I don't think Eddie will ever play with us. I don't think he wants to. I think he *wants* to be alone."

Then Eddie did something he'd never done before. He ran over to Alan and pulled on his arm, and he had the beginning of a small mischievous smile on his face. Billy said, "Do you know what I think? If Eddie *wanted* to be alone he wouldn't have done that. I don't think Eddie wants to be alone."

Eddie continued to stand there, right near the children, looking right at them, as though he wanted to tell them something.

"Eddie," Paul said, "What do you want? Please say what you want!" Eddie didn't answer.

Jimmy asked, "Eddie, do you want to play with us?"

Eddie stood there. He still did not say a thing.

"The summer is almost over, Eddie," Alan told him. "Soon it will be time to say goodbye again."

Charlie said, "Tell us if you want to play, Eddie. Say what you want!"

And then Eddie said, "I don't want to play." His very small smile got a little bigger. "I want to say hello," he said. And then he smiled a great, wide smile. It made his whole face look just beautiful.